D0460746

**For Oscar and Elias
with love, JN and LR**

**For Francesca
with love, SP**

PLUME
Published by the Penguin Group
Penguin Group (USA) LLC
375 Hudson Street

New York, New York 10014
USA I Canada I UK I Ireland I Australia I New Zealand I India I South Africa I China
penguin.com
A Penguin Random House Company

First published by Plume, a member of Penguin Group (USA) LLC, 2014

An earlier version of the text originally appeared in *The New Yorker*

P REGISTERED TRADEMARK—MARCA REGISTRADA

LIBRARY OF CONGRESS CATALOGING-IN-PUBLICATION DATA
Nessel, Jen.
Goodnight nanny-cam : a parody for modern parents / Jen Nessel and Lizzy Ratner; illustrated by Sara Pinto.
pages cm
ISBN 978-0-14-218070-9 (hardback)
1. Brown, Margaret Wise, 1910–1952—Parodies, imitations, etc. 2. Parenting—Humor.
I. Ratner, Lizzy. II. Pinto, Sara, illustrator.III. Title.
PS3614.E4985G66 2014
813'.6—dc23   2013030227

Set in Sasson Primary Std · Designed by Alissa Amell

GOODNIGHT NANNY-CAM

A PARODY FOR MODERN PARENTS

JEN NESSEL & LIZZY RATNER

ILLUSTRATED BY SARA PINTO

P

A PLUME BOOK

In the great green-certified room

There was a smart phone

And a silver spoon

And a picture of—

A high-contrast, brain-stimulating black-and-white moon

And there was a musical concert by Baby Mozart

And high window guards

And French flash cards

And a fireplace safety gate

And toys without phthalate

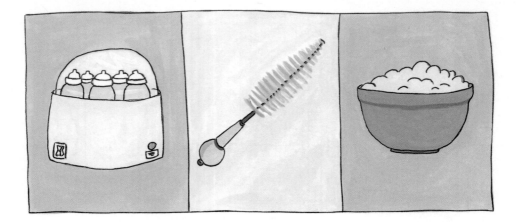

And a sterilizer and a bottle brush and a bowl full of organic mush

And a bilingual nanny who was whispering "hush"

Goodnight room

Goodnight recycled baby wipes with no perfume

Goodnight high-contrast black-and-white moon

Goodnight

baby monitor

And the nanny-cam

Goodnight French

flash cards

Bonne nuit petit canard

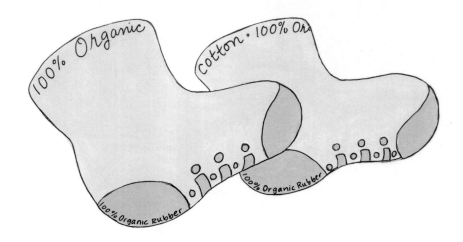

Goodnight nonslip socks

Handmade in VT with love ♡

And goodnight sustainable-wood blocks

Goodnight friends with unique, unusual names

And goodnight brain

development games

Goodnight digital archive of baby's first years

And goodnight Drs. Karp, Leach, Ferber, and Sears

Goodnight wipes warmer
and yoga mat, defibrillator
and sun hat

Goodnight sunscreen, sunglasses, sleep sack, outlet cap, sleep coach, speech coach, test coach, chess coach,

star charts, consumer reports, ergonomic sling, beeswax maple teething ring, vitamin D, anything with omega-3, French au pair, filtered air, and—